YARD SALE AT THE DEVIL'S PETTING ZOO

Poems by G.M.H. Thompson

Kansas City Spartan Press Missouri

Spartan Press
Kansas City, Missouri
spartanpresskc.com

Copyright (c) G.M.H. Thompson, 2018
First Edition 1 3 5 7 9 10 8 6 4 2
ISBN: 978-1-946642-82-0
LCCN: 2018964055

Design, edits and layout: Jason Ryberg
Cover image: G. M. H. Thompson
Author photo: Drew Sheafor
All rights reserved. No part of this publication may be reproduced or transmitted in any form or by any means, electronic or mechanical, including photocopying, recording or by info retrieval system, without prior written permission from the author.

Acknowledgments:

Spartan Press would like to thank Prospero's Books, The Fellowship of N-finite Jest, The Prospero Institute of Disquieted P/o/e/t/i/c/s, Will Leathem, Tom Wayne, Jeanette Powers, j. d. tulloch, Jon Bidwell, Jason Preu, Mark McClane, Tony Hayden and the whole Osage Arts Community.

Previous publication credits:

"In the Beginning" was first published by *Heart & Mind Zine*.
"Elegy for a Hare Deceased," & "I Am That" were all first published in annual poetry anthologies of Scurfpea Publishing, volumes 6 & 7.
"The Horse-Track" & "The Travels of an American" were both first published in *Helix*.
"Orchard," "Strawtrance," & "True Horror" were all first published in *Scifaikuest*.
"Ursula," "There's a Wild Cat" were all first published in *Bad Jacket*.
"Airy Anecdote" & "65 Million Years Ago" were both first published by *Anti-Heroin Chic*.
"A Lion Is Roaming the Streets of Milwaukee" was first published in *The Chariton Review*.

CONTENTS

In the Beginning / 1

The Horse-Track / 4

Elegy for a Hare Deceased / 6

The Travels of an American / 7

Orchard / 13

Strawtrance / 14

True Horror / 15

Ursula / 16

Narcissus Reflection / 18

Airy Anecdote / 23

I Am That / 24

There's a Wild Cat / 26

A Lion Is Roaming the Streets of Milwaukee / 28

Sonnet: God and My Right / 30

65 Million Years Ago: / 32

The Death of a Tree / 33

Island of a Bearded Man / 34

Boneyard Park, Champaign / 35

Harem / 36

Supermarket / 37

Honey Bee / 38

Jonagold / 39

Icebird / 40

Sidewalk Junk / 41

Diurnal Panoramic Wilderness / 42

Churchyard / 44

Karaoke Boho / 45

A Butterfly / 46

Havana / 48

The Drunken Bum / 49

Posthumous / 50

Postscript / 51

To a woman whose name ends with an "a."

In the Beginning

In the beginning, there was nothing but a blank canvas of infinite midnight. And then God said, *Let there be God.* And low and behold: God materialized out of the nothingness in all His heavenly glory.

And then God said, *Let there be Heaven, that I might live there and make it My abode.* And so it was— Heaven popped into existence with angelic spontaneity: a magnificent city of white marble mansions fitted with gold trim and floating upon wondrous clouds of sapphire and diamond. And God entered the eternal city and claimed the most marvelous of the mansions as His abode.

And then God said, *Let there be angels, that they might effect My will and exist to serve.* And so there were— glorious and beautiful in their appearance and in their souls. And God said unto the angels, *My children, you shall live in these mansions I have built for you and shall effect My will.* And the host of angels said that this was good and went into Heaven to live in the mansions and to serve the will of God.

And so, by the fourth day of pre-creation, God had put in three solid, sleepless days of heavy-duty conjuring and was starting to feel really burned-out.

He met with the Angel Gabriel and He said unto this angel, *Let everything else come into existence that should come into existence, for I am just really losing My concentration here, man, and am starting to space out real bad, if you can dig it. I mean . . . I mean . . . I could totally stand to just sort of . . . drift . . . off . . . to some place distant . . . and . . . just sort of chill . . . there, for a while . . . or something . . . . . .*

And the Angel Gabriel said unto God, *But Father, I am not omniscient or omnipotent, as are You. If You give me this weighty task of materializing everything else, many things will be that should not, and many more things will not that should be.*

But God was already gone . . . off . . . to some place distant . . . presumed to be chilling . . . there, for a while . . . or something . . . . . . and the Angel Gabriel was reluctantly forced into creating everything else he guessed was supposed to exist, making many mistakes in the process, just as he had tried to warn his ethereal Father he would.

Yet, surprisingly, the consequences for Gabriel's failures were but slight. For, you see, wherever that mysterious distant place was (or, possibly, is), it must have been very, very far away, very far away, indeed. Or, perhaps God so enjoyed Himself there that He just sort of . . .

forgot about things. Or, maybe it was just extremely hard to get to, that enigmatic realm that only He hath seen, and He just sort of . . . lost His way. Or, mayhap something else happened, something so profound only He knows about it, can know about it, can comprehend it. In any account, it is unknown precisely what happened to Him as a result of that vague . . . *drift . . . off . . . to some place distant . . .* , partaken on the fourth day, for, you see, God never came back.

The Horse-Track

His father earns the money
for the bread & the butter
& the mutton & the greens
& the salt & the pepper
& the little bitty oysters
that all deck the table
where little Jimmy sits
& that all, with time, will serve to make him strong.

    All from the track, from the track,
from the bloody, bloody track,
where his father is a jockey
and his mother does the dishes,
does the dishes,
does the bloody, bloody dishes;
it's all, it's all, it's all from the track.

    When little Jimmy walks five miles to school,
what's he see, what's he see when he enters that school?:
        horsehair desks & horse-chop lunches,
a horse-bone playground & Elmer's Glue.

        That's what he sees, that's what he sees,
        That's what he sees, that's what he sees,

That's what he sees, that's what he sees,
And there's more, too.

   For little Jimmy's school is paved in blood,
is paved in blood, is paved in blood.
Whose blood you ask?:
               That of a horse.

       'Cause taxpayer dollars are never there,
       & taxing the rich would just be unfair.
What's a poor southern county to do?:
       Put up a horse-track, race starts at two.

Elegy for a Hare Deceased

Walking to your birthday party,
I came across a rabbit, dead,
lying prone in the lifeless road,
and this was on Easter Sunday;—
a crowd of people stared at it
as flies picked at its jellied eyes
but I strolled by, oblivious— :
all sinners spurn their saviors thus.

The Travels of an American

He hitchhiked to LA
in three days hitchhiked to LA
& while he was there
lived off drive-in movie theaters,
t.v. dinners,
dime-store chronicles,
dreaming the whole time without sleep,
without rest,
without motion
or emotion,
desiring only
to desire something,
a desire unfulfilled
by the desert city,
the city that has everything
besides a conscience,
the city that blooms
like an opuntia rose
amidst the wasteland
of its own greatness,

& so he took the plane back
with cactus needles his only baggage
(carry-on, not checked),
leaving his troubles in LA

to wander the streets of gold
& opulent fountains
                        of dust
mundane ghosts of unpaid bills,
unfulfilled commitments, unfinished goals,
& came back empty of himself,

collapsing on the runway
after he got off the plane
& refusing to get up
for three days refusing to get up
even after the captain & stewardesses
asked him very nicely
refusing to get up,
& for three days
they could not fly aeroplanes
at that airport
& the air traffic controllers
were very sad
& so was America.

He rode the rails
to Chicago rode the rails
& met some girl,
but she wasn't his style,
she just wasn't his style—
he couldn't reconcile
himself to that fact:

she wasn't his style
& maybe there was no girl
& no Chicago, either,—
maybe he dreamed it all up
lying on the runway
after vacating LA,
which is where he maybe was still,
'cause she wasn't his style
& he just couldn't reconcile
himself to that fact,

& so he swam the Great Lakes
to Buffalo, & then
took the Erie Canal to New York City,
lying on his back like a barge
& bathing in all the chemicals
that washed off the farm fields
all the way down the Hudson
till he was large as a skyscraper
in New York City Harbor,
yet no one in New York City
seemed impressed by this
or even seemed to notice,

& he ate more hot dogs
than a bulimic Japanese man
at Nathan's Famous Hot Dog Eating Contest
& dated the Statue of Liberty

& played center for the Knicks,
but the Knicks still kept losing
& Liberty left him
for the Colossus of Rhodes
& all those hot dogs
gave him indigestion,

& so he sailed to Europe,
yet they wouldn't let him in
'cause he was a foreigner,
an American,
& so he converted to Islam
& snuck in among the Muslims
of Berlin
& had seven wives
in his harem,
each more amorous
than an angel's kiss,
Shahrazad, a sultan's dream,
waters of oblivion . . .

but then he woke up
& realized
he was still on the tarmac
after LA
& the president
of the United States
was standing before him

making a considerate
& really quite moving
speech about the importance
of not impeding air-traffic,

& there were protestors
lying on the runway with him
with chamomile hats
who said confused things
concerning Freedom
& cameras everywhere
& reporters asking
where he went to school
who was his favorite Power Ranger
why did he hate America
how he got addicted to penicillin
what was his position
                on group calisthenics

& the protestors
    told him he was a hero
& the president
    looked at him disapprovingly
& camera lightning
    struck every half-second
    & always the same place: him
& his publicity agent
    told him he was trending

    & his soothsayer
            told him his future was veiled
    & his talking head
            told him *Same as it ever was*
                     & it all made him so very tired

so he got up & walked home
in the violet light
of early evening
& checked his mailbox
& there was a postcard
from the Statue of Liberty
& she said that she missed him.

Orchard

      midnight
      dangling like apples:
corpses

Strawtrance

    emptiness
    corn field
    suicidal:
        strange transformation:
            scarecrow

True Horror

    no one ever sees
   the monster entirely
     out in the open
       and under the bed
      there is only
             a handful of dust

Ursula

When days are gray
& wolves creep up
onto the oars above the houses

when will they know
you want to see the lotus bloom
inside mermaid caves?

When dusk chills the heart
& the wreckers are all out
with hooks and lanterns

where will you go?
Down to the seashore
to collect fossils & oysters??

What will you hear?
Tales of Old Ahab
madly raging across the South Pacific??

What will you see?
Visions in the shadows
of sea monsters & succubae, Scylla & Charybdis??

What will you smell?
The bitter sea brine
duskily drinking the deck
amidst a sudden night squall??

What will you taste?
The blood of your enemies
as you lunge at them with cutlass,
crimson murder blazing fiercely in your eyes,
offsetting the flowering midnight??

What will you touch?
Tentacles of the deep,
fiendish arms of nether demons wrapped
wrapped
        wrapped
                wrapped around

wrapped around YOU
       and dragging you down, down, down
   down into the dark,
   down into the eternal dark
                    of the ocean's floor.

Narcissus Reflection

I'm a monster of will,
An animal of determination,
A being pure that burns to rule,
A prince of arrogance,
A king of confidence,
A lizard confidant,
A serpent of sibilance,
A snarling, saturnine destroyer,
A strangling sorcerer,
An antichrist & an anarchist,
A kiss of rage & irreverence,
A reckoning,
A wrecking crew,
A wrecking ball,
A revelation,
A revolution,
A backbench rebellion,
An institution
Of evolution
& devolution,
Of evil notions
& devil potions,
Pollutions,
Illusions,
& dull teardrop oceans.

I'm the wolf that bays at the doors of the apocalypse,
The minstrel that brays at the gates of insanity;
I'm the creature from the depths of the black lagoon,
The titular villain of every '50s B Movie,
The jester betraying his kingdom to doom,
The Joker staring down Batman's motorcycle with a
      machinegun in the middle of a darkly road,
The devil in the mind of Ivan Karamazov,
Fyodor Pavlovich, Nozdryov, Raskolnikov, &
Chichikov, too,

A pleasure-machine & a ticking time-bomb,
A cunning cardsharp & a rancorous fiend,
A liar, a lover, a rogue, and a fool,
A sailor on waves of madness & wonder,
A satirist weaving corruptions & plunders,
A saturnalian eruption & a going-under,
A scholarly knave of sadness and thunder,
A savior who braves the chances and blunders
Of satyrs & sitars & Sullas & rules.

I'm a bull in a chinashop of pure imagination,
A minotaur of crude imitation,
A labyrinth of rude indignation,
A touch of golden procrastination,
A lion roaming through webs & wastes of myth &
      magic,
A Roman ruin,

The ruins of time,
The mansions of eternity,
An illuminated manuscript,
The lost relics of Titus,
The Ark of the Covenant,
A Pandora's box,
A cloud serpent,
Quetzalcoatl
& the twilight of the gods.

I'm just analogue,
A whisper in the dark,
A lurker opaque,
A rumor obscure,
A wicked messenger,
A shadow,
A fantasy,
A reverie,
A dream,

A nightmare,
A dark horse,
A steeplechase,
A chariot race,
A pale steed,
A disease,
A patch of briers,
An off-key lyre,

A sultry mire,
A daemon's ire,
A idol's pyre,
A bomb's red wire;

I'm The Devil's Playground,
A minor djinn's petting zoo,
A menagerie of lies,
A Mephisophelean safari of maddening delusions,
A maniac in a mirror factory armed
with a sledgehammer,
A million years of warped & wicked luck,

Unstable & uneven,
Dazed & confused,
Slanted & enchanted,
A leprechaun & a lucky charm,

A platypus in Yugoslavia:
An anachronism,
A jaded schism,
A broken prism,
A plundered pyramid
Inside which eyes can only find
A cold stone coffin, empty:

I'm nothing,
Nobody,
A graveyard wasteland shattered throne,

A wandering wind, scattered unsown,
An idle saying, sources unknown,
An urban legend, suburbia grown,
An Apocrypha,
A chimera,
A charlatan,
A highwayman,
Scylla & Charybdis,
Alibaba & the Forty Thieves,
Odysseus & Achilles,
Aladdin's lamp & a flying carpet,
A Trojan horse & a Grecian god,
A hand of fate & a wheel of fortune,
A well where dwells some vague phantasm,
A rabbit hole & a wonderland.

> *I am the King of Crows*
> *I am the Prince of Dreams*
> *there's nothing that I know*
> *I'm never what I seem*

Airy Anecdote

—Did you hear about the balloon
 that got away?
It had a tether
 I don't know why
 & wherever it went
 it wrecked.
 The power lines it wrecked.
 the telephone wires it wrecked
 the t.v. towers it wrecked
Many
thousands of people
were without electricity
& I think finally
they shot it down.

I Am That

        I am a slaughterhouse;
        I am a factory of poisons.

        I am an oil spill;
        I am a pathogen that festers;
        I am a dinosaur of nightmares;
        I am a dragon mechanical.

        I am the death of a man,
        the death of a nation—
        a holocaust, a reckoning,
        the death of a star,
        the collapse of an astral plane,
        the shattering of worlds.

        I am that which comes last,
        that which finishes,
                          that which closes
every door—
        the period that punctuates with finality;
        I am the destroyer.

        I am the Twilight of the Gods
        and the earth reborn gentler
                          in reverent
hush.

If the radiance of a thousand suns
were to burst at once into the sky
that would be like the splendor of the Mighty One . . .
. . . I am become Death, the Shatterer of Worlds.

—The Bhagavad-Gita

There's a Wild Cat

. . . it had so many flowers
you couldn't see the leaves;
we had one with maybe
                twenty
                            flowers.

There's a wild cat out here,
there's a feral cat,
you know, sometimes when no one
cares about them & they're
on their own . . .
You know, I think I've seen that cat
a little while ago . . .
What do we do, just make our own sandwiches
why don't I just sit here on the corner
& you can make me a sandwich.
I only want one piece of bread, one piece of meat,
a little salad—
I've already had my pickle allowance . . .
Did you say you saw
that other feral cat:
there's two of them.
I don't know whose coffee this is.
We were all in Mammoth Cave
all of us

& you know
every kid had a bag with all their clothes . . .
I guess I lost my fork;
that's okay— :
we should just take all the forks here.
We took the train in Georgetown
with you;
why did they tear it down,
because it was dangerous
on the tracks?: —
take the chair behind you . . .
don't throw it away,
just put it here!
Do you know what the early people did with
       the buffalo?
they chased them to the end of the mesa
& then what happened to the buffalo?
they crashed to their death
& then they slaughtered them

A Lion Is Roaming the Streets of Milwaukee

A lion is roaming the streets of Milwaukee—
no one knows how it got there or where it came from,
maybe Nairobi, maybe east of Lake Baikal;
only five people have ever even seen it
& their accounts are shrouded in contradiction:
one sees tattered skin with scars like a blood zebra,
one sees a monument of muscles ruby eyed,
one sees lavish fur stretched taut over poles of bone,
one sees a wasted form much weaker than a lamb,
& the last just sees her own inadequacies
in the gleaming teeth & weary leer of the beast
as it retreats through the shadowy back alleys
& murky breweries that fog the land in beer—
a lion is roaming the streets of Milwaukee.

A lion is roaming the streets of Milwaukee
with eyes the size of windmills & fangs like glaciers
& a mane as grand as the Great Barrier Reef
& goliath ears & paws like tortured mountains
& claws like arctic winds & jaws like nebulae
& a heart that throbs with nuclear energy
& a growl that thunders with the furies of hell
& a monstrous mouth yawning like the cosmic void
& Atlas limbs leaping like an apocalypse
a lion is roaming the streets of Milwaukee.

A lion is roaming the streets of Milwaukee
with a ferocious hunger desiring to kill
& it's looking for you, frantically hunting you;
for your flesh alone this lion is wandering
& soon it will find you, no matter where you hide:
a lion is roaming the streets of Milwaukee.

Sonnet: God and My Right

It is my station in life
                      that I should not be second
    to any man
so when you ask me to bow
                      & kiss your ring
                                like
some obsequious
        courtier,
I will not do it
        & I care not
                if you ask for all the gold
in cheerless England
        & I care not
                if you hold me here
    till Kingdom come
        & I care not
                if you cut me
    with a thousand swords:
I will not do it

    for with the slightest will
                      I wrested
Cyprus from the hands of Rome
        & merely by drawing forth my sword
I breached the mighty walls of Acre

        & none but I have taught the cunning devil
Saladin defeat
        & I certainly will not consent
to lower myself
      to some
          German
              who has never seen
        Jerusalem:
I will not do it

        & if these treacherous, unholy chains
  would break
      I'd swiftly send to Hell the fool who names
me second
      with my strong right hand
    for I have no peer upon this earth
    & only God in Heaven
            ranks above my worth.

65 Million Years Ago:

Mais ou sont les neiges d'antan?
–François Villon, *Le Testament*, 336

Only bones remain
& petrified forests
& black seas in our automobiles

Today is a day of sacred ignorance
        a day of jejune decadence
        a day of blind ruination

We each & every one of us is lost

                        in forests of ruins
                          forests of decay
                    forests of sand & ashes
                  forests where we are weeping
  and know not why

Millennia are grinding to dust all around us
worlds disintegrating in the acid of our unbelief
universes torn to tatters through crass indifference
& there will be no redemption or reparation or
    reawakening.

The Death of a Tree

Thunder came & shivered the tree to deadwood— :
no one came to bury its shattered carcass
which became a playground to hordes of squirrels
climbing the dead boughs.

Grass grew thick to mourn for this fallen titan;—
no one thought to mow its laments to clippings,
making alley cats & raccoons a jungle
kingdom of downfall.

Garbage slept beside this enchanted forest;—
no one tried to throw it away for eons,—
ancient refuse carelessly littered by the
previous owners.

Empty doors stare blind at the broken body— :
no one lives here anymore— no one lives here

Island of a Bearded Man

They hate you, the small people
living in the small places,
content to moan like cattle
& lap the river of dung.

Others were to come after
& others will come before,
continuing the cycle
of cosmic retribution,

nihilism's nirvana,
solipsism's state of grace
is lost on you, Far Arden
a forgotten memory

& now you can't quite forget
that certain desperation
that comes when you least expect,
an angel's desolation,

an empty room of empty
chairs, & you can't quite sit down
'cause you can't quite see the point
& what's it all anyway.

Boneyard Park, Champaign

   lights on water dark:
artificial universe:
   nightsky ripples wings:

   geese imperial:
Canadian air grandeur:
   horns of war & dawn:

   mallards green, swans white,
grey heron: pensive, watching
   foaming staircase stream:

   concrete giants' teeth:
enchanted stone rings pagan,
   gaping maws of wet:

   algae river pool:
red-winged cattail rushes moss;
   bullfrog vanishes—

   sunset golden haze:
v-formations flying south;—
   twilight purple reigns.

Harem

water lilies bloom
beside a crystal fountain
in the Sultan's court

Supermarket

    death
        dreams among bananas:
       the Brazilian wandering spider

Honey Bee

    ebony & gold
newsprung flowers kissed to life:
            the earth reborn sweet

Jonagold

        cucumber cherry
autumn sun on a dirt road dies:
    my lost love's smile

Icebird

wings of coal
caress the snowman's
nose while awaiting gloves
bearing corn

Sidewalk Junk

an old television
sleeping on the curb:
me in seventy years

Diurnal Panoramic Wilderness

The sun
alights upon
the horizon at dawn
to blaze the sky & birth the day
anew.

Strange trees
are wreathed in mist
that gleams with ruby sheen
of eerie eye-pieced butterflies'
weird wings.

A herd
of antelope
meets death as in a dream:
abrupt the lion's jaws embrace
the throat.

Mountains
oppress the plain
with glares of crimson rage,
morose & rueful yet at peace
with pain.

A waste
of bones & fear
hyenas call a home
siestas in an amber daze
of night:

The sun
is wreathed in haze
& dies as in a dream:
morose & rueful yet at peace
with night.

Churchyard

        fuchsia waves,
    surf ivory:
           Botticelli's shell,
                fallen petals three

Karaoke Boho

    the crushed lime slice hovers limply
        in the rum, utterly
      submissive:
              an obscene monstrosity
              swims formaldehyde depths, dead

A Butterfly

      A pale green,
pale white
        butterfly
  flutters
      timidly
in the wind,
       seeming at certain times
              & in certain
                  places
      in the course of this
           idiotic
    song & dance number

to resemble a makeshift flag of truce,
a pitiful handkerchief stained pale green
by the puke of the brave captain who was
              taken

from this world by a stray shell-fragment just
seven minutes, fifty-two seconds beforehand,

leaving his men in

    shocked

      disarray

& greatly facilitating

the subsequent

    surrender

of the company.

Havana

    a burning eye
  wanders from the window
    yet sees nothing:
      a hand dreams on the sill
        in the tropical night, fondling a cigar

The Drunken Bum

       garbled profanities:
          the Tower of Babel
             both rising & slain,—
       the gesticulating voice
of the mad and homeless night

Posthumous

>to remember this
>just think of an opossum
>dead on the highway

Postscript

> *The ivory grains within an hourglass*
> *make a vertical archipelago*
> *within the ocean that is the moment*
> *yet in an hour's time will flow no more.*

The sky is white here, the sea breathes in & out
lapping the white sand with tongues of azure.
there are no clouds; they've taken all the clouds away
smells of palm & olive, a sun unseen & faint
the wind rustles gently through the rushes
& water lilies growing in the pool
that serves the garden like a pupil serves
an eye as I gaze out into nothingness
as the days drift by blind & silent in indifference
& endless as the stars that swim in midnight's sea.

The sky is white here; there are no clouds
the endless procession of triremes
that clutter the sea never seem to be sailing
anywhere, never seem to be moving even
leading me to wonder if they're even there
or if instead I've slipped into a dream
in the background pan flutes & lyre strings
& shades of blue & pink & orange all around
strange whispers: ancient kings, times to come
in a language I do not know yet understand

& scrolls innumerable in libraries marble
Ionian white imperial golden tresses
& the columns all Corinthians
& the soldiers all Spartans
& the academicians all Athenians.

And the sky is white here and there are no clouds
& there is a great weight upon my chest that throbs
& fills me with a terrifying happiness
& I feel as if awaiting something
& I know not what or when or why
& I only pray it be the will of God.

G.M.H. Thompson was born on February 15th, 1990, at about 12 midnight, in a hospital in Cleveland, Ohio.

This project was made possible, in part, by generous support from the Osage Arts Community.

Osage Arts Community provides temporary time, space and support for the creation of new artistic works in a retreat format, serving creative people of all kinds — visual artists, composers, poets, fiction and nonfiction writers. Located on a 152-acre farm in an isolated rural mountainside setting in Central Missouri and bordered by ¾ of a mile of the Gasconade River, OAC provides residencies to those working alone, as well as welcoming collaborative teams, offering living space and workspace in a country environment to emerging and mid-career artists. For more information, visit us at www.osageac.org

www.ingramcontent.com/pod-product-compliance
Lightning Source LLC
Chambersburg PA
CBHW030132100526
44591CB00009B/628